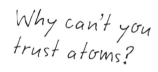

SCIENCE STUNTS
FUN FEATS OF PHYSICS

JORDAN D. BROWN

▪ ILLUSTRATED BY ANTHONY OWSLEY ▪

imagine!
Publishing

An Imagine Book
Published by Charlesbridge
85 Main Street, Watertown, MA 02472
(617) 926-0329
www.charlesbridge.com

Library of Congress Cataloging-in-Publication Data
Brown, Jordan, author.
 Science stunts : fun feats of physics / by Jordan D. Brown.
    pages cm
ISBN 978-1-62354-064-7 (reinforced for library use)
ISBN 978-1-60734-941-9 (ebook)
ISBN 978-1-60734-942-6 (ebook pdf)
1. Physics–Experiments–Juvenile literature.
2. Science–Experiments–Juvenile literature. I. Title.

QC26.B76 2016
530.078–dc23   2014045661

10 9 8 7 6 5 4 3 2 1

For information about custom editions, special sales,
premium and corporate purchases, please contact
Charlesbridge Publishing at specialsales@charlesbridge.com

For my daughter, Olivia,
who inspires me with her infinite curiosity, creativity, and compassion.

- -

Acknowledgments

Thanks to the terrific team that pooled their talents to bring this book to life. I'm grateful to editor Kate Hurley for her encouragement, meticulous attention to detail, and for reminding me of the writer's law of inertia: "a manuscript in motion stays in motion." It was a pleasure collaborating again with Anthony Owsley. His delightful illustrations not only add a huge fun factor, but also bring clarity to the experiments. Many thanks to designer Melissa Gerber for bringing all the elements together so beautifully and skillfully. I'm also grateful to science teacher Stuart Miles for reading the manuscript for accuracy and accessibility to young scientists, and to Joe Rhatigan for helping out while Kate was occupied with all things Teddy. Thanks, too, to Charles Nurnberg for asking me to write another hands-on science book for kids.

Special thanks to my wonderful family. I'm grateful to my beautiful wife, Ellen, for her love and support; my son, Finian, for his boundless energy as a creative problem solver; and my parents, Eileen and Stephen Brown, who sparked my interest in science by taking me to innovative science museums and who continue to encourage my creative efforts.

A quick word to the ghosts of Newton, Galileo, and Einstein: Thanks for letting me mess with your legacies! If there are any errors between these covers, I blame you guys for not jumping in a time machine and correcting them.

- -

Doing experiments and exploring science can be so much fun! I want you to get hooked on physics and have a great time as you create your own marshmallow catapult, set off a chain reaction with wooden sticks, and make your own electromagnet. What I *don't* want is for anyone reading this book to get injured, damage any household items, or get in trouble because they didn't read and respect the important safety rules. So read the rules NOW. The publisher's pesky lawyers would like to point out that the author and the publisher are not responsible for the use or misuse of any experiment in this book.

Some of the experiments require the help of a responsible grown-up, a.k.a. your Adult Sidekick.

When you see this picture, be aware that these experiments involve potentially dangerous materials, such as fire, glass, or electricity. Don't do these experiments without your Adult Sidekick, and be sure to wear the appropriate safety gear. Doing fun physics feats is a fantastic way to enjoy time together, so stick to the rules and you'll have a blast!

IMPORTANT SAFETY RULES & TIPS

- Read all the directions before you start. That way you know what you're getting into! You'll also know what props to have ready.

- If you see "Adult Sidekick" listed in the Props of an experiment, this means you must have a responsible grown-up with you. You don't want to end up causing a major problem in the name of fun.

- Wear eye protection any time the instructions tell you to, or when you think your eyes might get injured. You can buy inexpensive safety glasses at most hardware stores. If you already wear eyeglasses, you should be fine.

- Wash your hands after working with chemicals (such as the clear nail polish on page 62).

CONTENTS

THE MAGIC OF SCIENCE AND THE SCIENCE OF MAGIC

"Magic's just science that we don't understand yet."
—Arthur C. Clarke, writer and inventor

"If you're scientifically literate, the world looks very different to you."
—Neil deGrasse Tyson, astrophysicist

I've loved doing science experiments since I was little. When I was about ten, my parents encouraged this passion by taking me to science museums, such as the Ontario Science Centre in Toronto and the Exploratorium in San Francisco. I had a marvelous time pressing buttons, lifting levers, cranking gears, creating sparks, and so much more. Around that age, I also became very interested in magic and loved to perform card tricks, make balls float, and cause coins to vanish. I even performed shows at birthday parties as the Amazing Nadroj (my first name backward) and the Great Jordini (after my hero, Houdini). So, many years later, when I was asked to write a book for kids on physics that featured entertaining "magical" experiments, I jumped at the chance.

What is physics, anyway? It's a branch of science that explores topics such as motion, energy, magnetism, electricity, light, and sound. Physicists study itty-bitty things, like atoms, as well as super big objects, like stars, planets, and even galaxies. Physicists ask mind-blowing questions such as, "What if there were no gravity?" "What if you could travel at the speed of light?" and "What would happen if I dropped this watermelon off a tall building?"

As you play around with physics in this book, you'll learn some amazing science-based tricks and experiments that you can share with your friends and family. I also hope that you'll enjoy showing off what you learn in "the Science Behind the Stunts."

It's time to turn things over to the host of this book, a curious and enthusiastic scientist and showman whose enthusiasm for physics is unmatched. I present to you the one, the only . . . Dr. Dazz!

Welcome to my world of physics,
Where science and showbiz mix!
Every cool experiment
Is fueled with fun and merriment.
You'll get smarter as you
do these stunts and tricks!

Greetings! I'm here to help you explore the wonders of science. My full name is Dr. David Alva Leonardo Amadeus Franklin Maxwell Dazzleberry (my parents had a sense of humor), but most people call me **DR. DAZZ**. I'm a professional physicist and magician, and I can't wait to take you on a journey through the world of physics!

In this book, there are twenty-five experiments for you to try. After you've tried each science stunt, my trusty team of phenomenal physicists will explain how it works. Speaking of which, it's time to introduce these science bigwigs. They are not only my close, personal friends, but also have changed the way we look at the world.

First, here's a guy so incredibly influential that he earned the title "the Father of Modern Science." He was born in Italy in 1564, and his intense curiosity inspired him to study science, math, music, art, and more. He supported the then radical idea that the Earth orbits the sun, rather than the other way around. Give it up for **GALILEO GALILEI**!

Next up, a science superstar who was the brains behind some of the biggest ideas in modern physics. Born on a farm in 1642 in England, this chap's brilliant discoveries blew the minds of many of the scientists of his time. His famous laws of motion and gravity solved mysteries about the universe. By carefully testing his hypotheses, he made many important discoveries about color, light, rainbows, and soap bubbles. Let's hear it for **SIR ISAAC NEWTON**!

Last but not least, here's a science genius who was born in Germany in 1879. His famous equation, $E=MC^2$, has helped us understand how the universe works. His mind-blowing theory of relativity changed our ideas of time, space, light, and gravity. In his free time, he loved to play violin and go sailing. It's my pleasure and honor to present to you, **ALBERT EINSTEIN**!

Now turn the page, grab your props, and get experimenting!

GALILEO GALILEI   **SIR ISAAC NEWTON**   **ALBERT EINSTEIN**

CHAPTER 1

TAKE *THAT*, GRAVITY!

> Toss an apple in the air;
> It soon comes down, of course.
> Because the Earth has gravity—
> A cool attractive force!

Whoa! Balancing all this stuff is tricky! Gravity is working against me. As you probably know, gravity is the invisible force that pulls you back to the ground when you jump in the air. Gravity is also the force that keeps the oceans from flying off into space. Without gravity, the moon wouldn't circle the Earth, the Earth wouldn't orbit the sun, and the whole universe would go *kablooey* (to use the scientific term). I could gush about gravity for hours, but as you can see, I'm kind of busy right now—so let's hear from Sir Newt before our first stunt.

NEWTON EXPLAINS GRAVITY

Gravity is one of my all-time favorite subjects. Back in 1687, I—the great Sir Isaac Newton—came up with my universal law of gravitation and wrote about it in my book *The Principia* (a brilliant title, if I do say so myself!). I'm sure you've read it many times and have given it as birthday gifts to all your friends. But I digress. I'd love to read that section to you in the original Latin and show you my complicated mathematical formula, but Dr. Dazz has sadly informed me that would be a bad idea, so I'll give you the big picture instead.

My law about gravity basically says this: **Gravity** is an invisible force that pulls all objects in the universe toward one another. In other words, *everything* has gravity. The more massive and closer an object is, the more pulling power it has. Since the Earth is the largest thing around us, when we jump in the air, we are pulled down to the ground. You can't feel it, but your body's gravity is also pulling up on the Earth. In the solar system, the force of gravity is what keeps all the planets orbiting the sun and keeps moons orbiting the planets. If there were no gravity, the universe would be chaos, I tell you, CHAOS.

WOOD BLOCK BAFFLER

· THE TRICK ·

Build a sculpture that balances on one thin block and looks like it should topple over!

· PROPS ·

- 14 identical rectangular building blocks (*must* be identical)
- smooth, flat surface

· WHAT TO DO ·

1. Balance two blocks vertically, and then place a third block horizontally across the top. Nudge this third block slightly to the left so one end hangs over the left vertical block.

2. Stand a fourth block vertically on the right edge of the third block to form a backward L shape.

3. Place a fifth block horizontally on top of the third block, up against the vertical fourth block. Its left end should hang out over the third block.

4. Repeat Steps 2 and 3 for the rest of the blocks.

5. Carefully remove the bottom vertical block on the right side. The tower should stand without toppling over. As you remove the bottom right block, you might need to gently adjust the blocks above it, to the left or right, to keep things in balance.

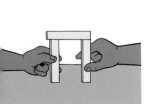

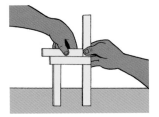

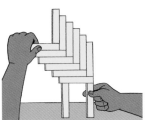

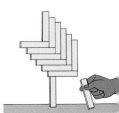

step 1   step 2   step 3   step 4   step 5

BONUS CHALLENGE

Find fourteen other identical rectangular objects to try balancing in this pattern. You could try cereal boxes (but don't do it in a supermarket!), dominoes, or even paperback books. The key is making sure that there is equal weight on both sides of the vertical block that will be holding up the whole shebang, so the items *must* be identical in size and shape (or very similar).

The Science Behind the Stunt

Bravo, bravo! Your tower is *fantastico*. You're quite a *scienziato*—that's Italian for *scientist*. Permit me to introduce myself: I am Galileo Galilei. I was born in Pisa, Italy, where there's a famous tower. Perhaps you've heard of it—the Leaning Tower of Pisa. It has been around for more than eight hundred years! They planned to build it straight up, but the ground below was too soft, so it tilted. One reason the tower hasn't toppled over is that its **center of gravity** is in the middle of the building, not too high up. The center of gravity is the spot where all the weight of an object is concentrated. When you spin a top and it doesn't wobble, it is spinning on its center of gravity.

The tower stunt works because as you add blocks to the tower, this gradually moves its center of gravity from right to left. By the time it was done, the tower was perfectly balanced over the bottom *left* block, so you could easily remove the bottom *right* block because it was no longer needed for support.

CENTER OF GRAVITY

 • • • A NOSE FOR GRAVITY • • •

· THE TRICK ·

Balance a pencil on your nose and count to ten.

· PROPS ·

- new, unsharpened pencil
- 1 piece of sturdy wire, about 6 inches long
- 2 wooden clothespins
- your nose
- a friend's nose

· WHAT TO DO ·

1. How long do you think you can balance a pencil vertically on your nose? Try it! Unless you're a professional circus performer, the pencil will probably fall off right away. To help balance the pencil, you're going to build a fun scientific thingamabob.

2. Pull the wire into a straight line and place the pencil on the center of it, about 1 inch below the eraser. Wrap the left side of the wire across the pencil, then wrap the right side of the wire across in the other direction. This should hold it tightly around the pencil. (If the wire slips, wrap it around another time.)

3. Hold the pencil vertically with the eraser at the bottom, and bend the ends of the wire down in a slight curve. Then attach a clothespin to each end of the wire, with the closed parts of the pins facing up. Ta-da! You're done building. Now it's time to experiment.

4. Try balancing the eraser end of the pencil on the tip of your nose, with the wires and clothespins hanging down on the sides. To make it work, you may need to bend the wire a little more, adjust the position of the clothespins, or slide the wrapped wire downward so it's closer to the eraser end. Once you get the pencil to balance, see if you can keep it on your nose for at least ten seconds. Have a contest with a friend to see who can balance it longer!

5. As an extra experiment, see what happens if you tighten the wire around the *middle* of the pencil. Can you still balance the pencil on your nose or finger? Why do you think the pencil balances better when the weights are lower?

Excellent experimenting! Simply cracking! I must say that I—the ingenious Sir Isaac Newton—am most impressed with your perseverance and patience. The secret of this stunt is the same physics idea that my esteemed colleague Galileo told you about: the center of gravity (which most serious scientists call "center of mass"). You might think that *my* genius brain came up with this concept, but the credit goes to Archimedes, a mathematician in ancient Greece.

NEWTON

To understand how this trick works, keep in mind this important idea: *The lower an object's center of gravity, the easier it is to balance it.* Try this little experiment with an unsharpened pencil: Hold it horizontally and balance it on one finger. The spot on the pencil right above your finger is the pencil's center of gravity. Now turn the pencil vertically and try balancing it again on your finger, with the eraser side down. Not easy to do! That's because the pencil's center of gravity is now far above the eraser end. But when you add that delightful thingamabob—the wire and clothespins—you add weight to the pencil. This lowers the center of gravity to below your finger, so you can easily balance it.

PHYSICS IN ACTION
A Grand Balancing Act

Daredevil Nik Wallenda calls himself the King of the High Wire. In 2013, he supported that title by doing an amazing balancing stunt: Thirteen million people watched on TV as he walked 1,400 feet across a two-inch steel cable over a gorge near the Grand Canyon. What's more, he didn't have a safety net, and there were high winds whipping around him! How did he pull off this feat? In addition to many years of practice, a remarkable sense of balance, and incredible focus, Wallenda was helped by physics. In particular, as he walked across the gorge, he carried a forty-pound metal pole. This pole lowered his center of gravity and made it easier for him to balance. Human bodies are normally top-heavy: Two-thirds of our weight is in the top part of our bodies. By carrying the heavy metal pole as he walked on the wire, Wallenda lowered his center of gravity.

MAY THE FORKS BE WITH YOU

· THE TRICK ·

Two heavy forks, held up only by a thin toothpick, appear to defy gravity.

· PROPS ·

- 2 metal forks, the heavier the better
- thick chunk of carrot, about 2 inches long
- toothpick
- tall, heavy glass

· WHAT TO DO ·

1. Connect the two forks by pressing them into opposite ends of the carrot chunk, with the tines facing each other.

2. Stick a toothpick in the side of the carrot, in between the two forks.

3. Balance the toothpick on the edge of the glass with approximately half the toothpick sticking out in each direction. It will probably take practice to get it just right.

Erstaunlich! That's German for *amazing*. This trick is the sort of thing I would have loved when I was a little stinker growing up in Munich. It works because there's a black hole inside the glass that sucks the carrot with its powerful gravity. Just kidding! The secret to this trick is that the center of gravity is in an unexpected place—in the empty space between the two forks. When an object is long and flat, like a yardstick, the center of gravity is *on* the stick, in the very middle. But in this experiment, the center of gravity is on an imaginary line formed by the arc of the two forks stuck to the carrot. Look at the dotted line in the diagram below. The midpoint of that line, where the toothpick sits, is the center of gravity.

Heavier forks work better than lighter forks because they have more weight on both ends, which lowers the center of gravity (like the tightrope walker on page 13!).

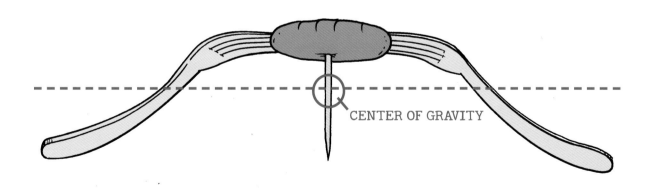

CENTER OF GRAVITY

HAMMER BALANCING ACT

· THE TRICK ·

Make a ruler stick *way* off the edge
of a table—without falling off!

· PROPS ·

- hammer
- 12-inch wooden or metal ruler
- pillow
- long, thick rubber band (or 6- to
  8-inch piece of string tied in a loop)
- table

· WHAT TO DO ·

1. Find the ruler's center of gravity: Put it on the table with the edge sticking off a bit. How far can you push the ruler off the end before it falls off the table? Probably about halfway (six inches). That's because the ruler's center of gravity is right in the middle, since its weight is evenly distributed.

2. Now compare the hammer's center of gravity with the ruler's. For safety, put a pillow near the edge of the table, right below where you'll be pushing off the hammer. Put the hammer on the table with the head right at the edge. Carefully observe the hammer as you *slowly* push it from the bottom of the handle off the table, until it falls and hits the pillow. (Make sure it doesn't land on your foot!) How much of the hammer was off the table when it fell? You'll discover that its center of gravity is not in the middle of its handle, but much closer to the head, which is the heaviest, most massive part.

3. Now for the stunt: Loop the rubber band around the hammer (close to the head) and stick one end of the ruler in the other end of the rubber band.

4. Hold the hammer as you place about 1 inch of the ruler on the table edge. The rubber band should hang from the ruler about an inch from the table. The handle of the hammer will press against the ruler.

5. Little by little, adjust the hammer, rubber band, and ruler until the ruler is sticking off the table as far as possible. See if you can get the ruler to balance with just ¼ inch resting on the table.

Jolly good show! A splendid display of physics! To understand why this delightful trick works, think about seesaws. When you and a friend who weighs about the same as you sit on opposite ends of a seesaw, it balances, right? But if a lighter friend sits on the other end, you have to scooch forward in order to get the seesaw perfectly horizontal again. In this trick, as you move the ruler off the table, you need something heavy to balance the other side. And *that*, my curious friend, is what the hammer does! Gravity pulls the hammer's head downward, which applies extra force to the tip of the ruler that is balancing on the table. In physics, the hammer is called a counterweight.

This trick is fun because it fools our noggins. Normally, a ruler couldn't stick out so far from a table without falling off. Also, many objects, like pencils and books and oranges, have consistent weight throughout. In the case of the hammer, the head is *much* heavier than the handle. The force of gravity pulls down on the hammer, which puts lots of pressure just where you want it—on the bit of the ruler still on the table.

LOOK OUT BELOW!

I, Galileo, love doing experiments with gravity. In one of my favorite stories about myself, I did an experiment at the top of the Leaning Tower of Pisa in Italy in the 1590s. I dropped two different-size metal balls at the same time. One was big and heavy, the other smaller and lighter. Most people thought that the heavy ball would fall faster and hit the ground first. But—surprise!—both balls hit the ground at the *same time*. That's because gravity pulls down all objects at the same rate.

Now, on Earth, some light objects fall slower than heavy objects. If you drop a rock and a piece of paper, what happens? That's right: The rock hits the ground before the paper floats down. This is because gravity isn't the *only* force acting on the objects. Even though gravity pulled down the rock and the paper at the same rate, the force of air resistance slowed down the paper's fall.

On the moon—*luna* in Italian—there is no air resistance, so light and heavy objects fall at the same rate. In the 1970s, an astronaut on the moon held up a hammer and a feather at the same height, then let go. Guess what? They landed at the same time! If you go online and search for "Apollo 15" and "hammer and feather," you can see a video of this lunar experiment.

CHAPTER 2

THE MAGIC OF MOTION

When something bursts with motion,
You might wonder, What's the cause?
You'll soon see it's energy,
Like in Newton's laws!
If you're patient and you practice,
Your friends will drop their jaws.
They'll shower you with compliments
And give you loud applause.

It's time to get your mojo into motion! All the stunts and tricks in this chapter will help you learn some scientific laws about how things moooooove. You'll witness the power of a pendulum, experience the thrill of a chain reaction, and become a whiz at centripetal force. Right now, this big rubber band is LOADED with energy. As soon as my team of phenomenal physicists lets go, I'm going to fly on the ride of my life! Wait, where are the crash pillows? Sir Newt, wasn't it your job to set them up? Uh-oh.

· THE TRICK ·

Heavy metal nuts should crash to the ground—but they don't.

· PROPS ·

- 15 hex nuts or washers (all the same size)
- piece of string, about 18 inches long

· WHAT TO DO ·

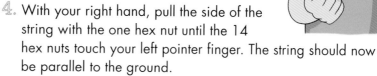

1. Slide 14 hex nuts onto one end of the string and tie a knot to secure them into a loop.

2. Slide the last hex nut onto the other end of the string and tie a knot to hold it in place.

3. Hold the end of the string with one hex nut in your right hand. Dangle the rest of the string over the pointer finger of your left hand.

4. With your right hand, pull the side of the string with the one hex nut until the 14 hex nuts touch your left pointer finger. The string should now be parallel to the ground.

5. Say some magic science words, like "Presto Hawking!" or "Abraca Higgs boson!" Then, holding your left hand still, let go of the side with one hex nut. The string won't crash to the ground, but instead will wrap around your left pointer finger. Can you figure out why?

Meraviglioso! (That's Italian for *wonderful*.) This trick works because of three of my favorite science topics: pendulums, gravity, and friction. And who better to teach you such things than me, Galileo, your very own *genio affascinante*? (That's Italian for *charming genius*.) A **pendulum** is something that swings back and forth from a fixed point—like a playground swing. Gravity, as you know, is the invisible force that pulls things down to the Earth. And **friction** is the force that resists motion when two objects rub together. When you run in your socks and slide on a smooth floor, you keep moving because there isn't much friction. If you did the same thing in hiking boots on a rough rug, you'd stop almost instantly because of all the friction.

GALILEO

So what do pendulums, gravity, and friction have to do with this trick? When you let go of the lighter end of the string, the heavier end is pulled down by gravity. You think gravity is going to win and make the heavy nuts hit the ground, but two things happen first: The fast downward pulling motion causes the light end of the string to swing very quickly back and forth. In other words, it becomes a pendulum. This happens so fast, it's hard to see. With each swing, the end of the string with the single nut builds up energy, swinging higher and higher until it wraps around the top of your finger. When the string wraps around your finger, friction stops it from slipping off. It locks in place and prevents the nuts from falling.

Do you think this trick would work if you had only ten hex nuts at one end of the string? Experiment and explore the answer. (Just not over your grandma's favorite glass table.)

· THE TRICK ·

Create a catapult that will launch mini marshmallows into your buddy's mouth.

· PROPS ·

- 9 wooden craft sticks or tongue depressors (wider than Popsicle sticks)
- about 10 rubber bands
- sturdy plastic spoon
- mini marshmallows

· WHAT TO DO ·

1. Stack seven craft sticks and wrap a rubber band tightly around each end.

2. Take two more craft sticks and wrap a rubber band tightly around one end. Lift the top stick of the unwrapped end and insert the bundle of sticks from Step 1 horizontally in between the two sticks.

3. Wrap one or two rubber bands in a crisscross pattern to lock the bundle of seven sticks in between the two sticks. Press the seven-stick bundle as close to the wrapped end of the two sticks as possible.

4. Use two rubber bands to attach the plastic spoon to the top stick, one near the base of the spoon and one at the middle of it.

5. It's launch time! Firmly hold the bottom end of the launcher on the table with one hand, put a mini marshmallow into the plastic spoon, pull back the spoon, and then let it go and watch the marshmallow fly! See how far you can launch it. Try to aim the marshmallow into a friend's mouth. Experiment with your catapult by using different numbers of sticks in the bundle, or see what happens when you slide the bundle closer or farther away from the rubber-banded end of the two sticks.

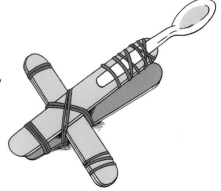

Good show, my inquisitive pupil! I say, never has there been a tastier projectile! As we say in Latin, *S'mores sunt delectamentum, sed regula catapultae.* That means, "S'mores are delicious, but catapults rule." Catapults are marvelous machines for demonstrating three extremely fabulous and famous laws of motion. These laws were discovered by a brilliant chap with unparalleled insight, remarkable skill, and stunning good looks: ahem—ME. My three laws describe how and why objects move. I'll skip past all the beautiful math and formulas and provide you with the basics.

NEWTON

My **first law of motion** says that moving objects keep moving, in a straight line at the same speed, unless a force slows them down or speeds them up or makes them change direction. My first law also says that still objects will *not* move unless a force makes them. Scientists often call this law the law of inertia. **Inertia** is the idea that objects like to keep doing what they're doing. In other words, moving things tend to keep moving, and still things usually stay still. The marshmallow in your catapult follows this law. It stays still in the spoon until a force (you) launches it with the catapult, then *ZIIIIING!* Off it goes. It travels through the air, going, going, going . . . until gravity pulls it down, or it hits your little sister in the head. (Serves her right for barging into the room!) The marshmallow's speed also slows down because of friction from the air it is moving through. If you were to fling a marshmallow with your catapult in outer space, where there is no air resistance, the marshmallow would keep going in a straight line, at the same speed, FOREVER!

My **second law of motion** says the speed that a moving object will travel depends on two things: (1) how heavy it is (its mass) and (2) how much force is put on it. This law explains why it takes much more effort to toss a bowling ball than a Ping-Pong ball. With your catapult, you can demonstrate that the amount of force you use to pull back on the spoon will affect how far the marshmallow will go. If you pull back the spoon a little bit, the marshmallow only goes a short distance. But if you pull back the spoon as far as the rubber band will let you, then the marshmallow will travel much farther. Here's an experiment to try: Fling a mini marshmallow and a regular-size marshmallow with the same amount of force and see which one travels farther. You should find that the regular marshmallow doesn't go as far.

Finally, my **third law of motion** states that for every action, there is an equal and opposite reaction. When you pull back the spoon (the action), the spoon pushes back on your fingers. This builds up energy, which gets released in the opposite direction when you let go and the spoon flings forward (the reaction). The more force that's used to pull the spoon backward, the greater the force the spoon will push forward, and the greater the distance the marshmallow will fly. (Beware: If the marshmallow hits an unsuspecting victim, you might get what scientists call an *over*reaction!)

SCIENTISTS AT PLAY
PUMPKINS AWAY!

The week after Halloween, there are a lot of extra pumpkins hanging around. Well, this situation and the fact that scientists love to make big things fly through the air leads to a wild event in Delaware. It's known as Punkin Chunkin, and the goal is to build a catapult or other device that launches an eight- to ten-pound pumpkin as far as possible. Like the marshmallow flinger, these machines demonstrate Newton's laws of motion. Some contestants build a trebuchet (treh-byoo-SHET), which is a type of catapult that uses a counterweight to add force. Pumpkins have been launched over one thousand feet!

··· PENNY IN ORBIT ···

· THE TRICK ·

Make a penny whirl around the inside of a balloon—like a planet orbiting the sun.

· PROPS ·

- penny
- balloon (preferably clear latex)

· WHAT TO DO ·

1. Push the penny into the mouth of the balloon and let it fall to the bottom. (If you can find a clear latex balloon, you'll be able to see better what happens inside, but any balloon will work.)

2. Blow air into the balloon until you can start to see inside it. Be careful not to overinflate it or it will pop during the experiment. And make sure to blow it up with your face looking down at the floor so the penny doesn't fall back into your mouth! Tie off the balloon.

3. Grip the balloon so the knot is touching your palm and your palm is facedown. Gently wiggle the balloon in a little circle by rotating your wrist. At first, you'll hear the penny bouncing around inside. Keep spinning the balloon in the same direction, getting faster and faster.

4. Once you see the penny moving around inside the balloon on its edge, use your other hand to grab onto the bottom of the balloon and hold it in place. This will quickly stop the balloon's motion. Even though the balloon is no longer spinning, the penny will continue on its circular path for a long time.

5. Grab a friend and see who can get the penny to spin around the longest before it stops. You can also experiment with different-size coins to see if they behave differently than the penny.

einstein

Gefälschte Deutsche wort! That's German for *fake German word.* But enough silliness! That experiment not only made my head spin, it's a wonderful example of my pal Newton's first law. You know, the one about inertia. Newton said that moving things keep moving until a force slows them down. If there's little friction, things keep moving. The inside of the balloon is made of a very smooth material, and the edge of the penny is also smooth. So when the penny slides along the inside of the balloon, there's very little friction. What eventually makes the penny move downward, of course, is the force of gravity.

The force that keeps the penny going around and around is centripetal force. **Centripetal force** presses inward and makes an object moving on a curved path keep turning as it goes around. Any circular motion would not be possible without this force. It keeps riders in their seats as they go around a roller coaster loop. Here's something fun to do outside: Hold a bucket of water in one hand and swing it in a big circle. If you swing fast enough, centripetal force will not let the water fall out of the bucket!

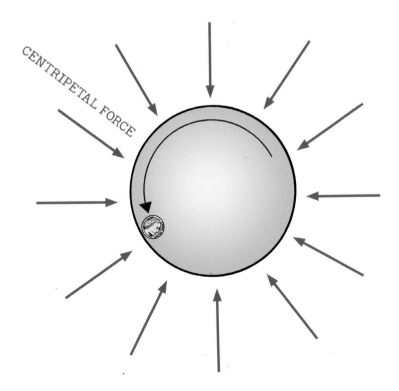

CENTRIPETAL FORCE

···STICK···STICK···BOOM!···

adult sidekick needed

· THE TRICK ·

Build a chain reaction that will cause wooden sticks to fly into the air!

· PROPS ·

- 30 or more wooden craft sticks or tongue depressors (**not** Popsicle sticks)
- floor with carpet or thick rug
- marker (to label sticks)
- safety glasses
- paper or plastic cups (optional)
- Adult Sidekick

NOTE: This trick takes LOTS of patience and practice, but the results are AMAZING. In fact, before you start, you and your Adult Sidekick should go online and watch a video of a "stick chain reaction."

· WHAT TO DO ·

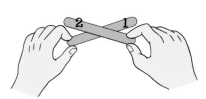

1. Number ten sticks 1 through 10 with a marker. Put the numbers near the middle so you can see them as you weave the sticks together. The numbers make it much easier to keep track of the different sticks and follow the pictures here. Once you're a pro, you can skip the numbers!

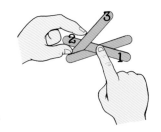

2. Put on your safety glasses to protect your eyes. (Your Adult Sidekick should do the same.)

3. Working on a carpet or thick rug, put Stick 1 and Stick 2 into an X pattern, with 2 on top of 1. Note that the two ends of the sticks are about a thumb's width apart.

4. Add Stick 3 to the **left** side. Press down in the middle of the X with your right finger and squeeze Stick 3 vertically under Stick 1 and over Stick 2.

5. While keeping your right finger on the X, use your left finger to slide Stick 3 down to the right until its lower corner comes out a bit behind Stick 1. Use your left hand to hold down Stick 3 over Stick 2.

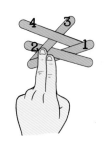

6. Add Stick 4 to the **right** side. Press down in the middle of Stick 3 with your left finger and squeeze Stick 4 vertically under Stick 1 and over Stick 3.

7. When you're done, rotate Stick 4 down to the left, so it is parallel with Stick 2, and is positioned a little to the left of Stick 2.

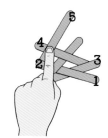

8. Hold down Stick 4 with your right finger. Add Stick 5 to the **left** side, putting it under Stick 2 and over Stick 4, so that Stick 5 is parallel to Stick 3. Use your left pointer to hold Stick 5 in place.

9. Add Stick 6 on the **right** side, inserting it under Stick 3 and over Stick 5, so that Stick 6 is parallel to Stick 4. Use your right pointer finger to hold Stick 6 in place.

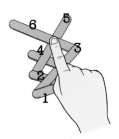

10. Keep adding sticks, alternating left side and right side, until you've added as many sticks as you'd like. When you add more sticks, always add them under one stick and over another near it. *Don't get discouraged* if you have a hard time setting up this grid. While learning to make it, you'll sometimes make mistakes and have to start over.

11. To temporarily lock the stick chain while you're working, slide the last stick you added underneath the stick right next to it. To unlock, reverse this process, being sure to hold down the X below where the locking stick was added. You should lock them like this from time to time and make sure the grid is not sticking to the carpet by gently lifting it up.

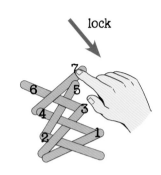

12. After you've finished building the chain, lock off the last stick as noted in Step 11.

13. When you're ready to set off the stick chain, remove Stick 1 while holding down Stick 3. Then step back and watch the magic!

14. For added fun, you can put a pyramid of paper or plastic cups on top of the end of the stick chain. They will fly into the air when you set off the reaction! If you're even more ambitious, look online to see examples of stick chains that use hundreds, and even *thousands*, of sticks and try to replicate them!

The Science Behind the Stunt

I applaud your determination and persistence! But how does it work? The secret is that when the sticks are woven together, they bend slightly, so they store up energy. When one stick is pressed down over another stick and held in place by yet another stick, this prevents the energy from escaping. Think of when you stretch out a rubber band: Before you let it go, the energy is "trapped" in the band. This is called **potential energy**. When you release the band, this potential energy turns into **kinetic energy**, or moving energy. On a roller coaster ride, when you're on the tallest hill, you have lots of potential energy. As the coaster car zooms downhill due to gravity, the car's potential energy quickly becomes kinetic energy. As the car moves uphill, kinetic energy transfers to potential energy. In this experiment, the kinetic energy of one stick releases the potential energy of the next stick, causing a **chain reaction**. It's similar to when you set up dominoes vertically in a long line, then tap the first one to make them all topple, one by one. This stick experiment also illustrates my pal Newton's second law, which states that the speed at which the sticks explode depends on the force that the sticks are putting on one another. The more pressure you can build, the stronger the force that will be released.

SCIENTISTS AT PLAY

CRAZY CONTRAPTIONS

If you're looking for the easiest way to hammer a nail or water a plant, you should definitely *not* look to the Rube Goldberg Machine Contest at Purdue University. The mission of this contest is to create a wild, wacky machine that uses as many silly steps as possible to accomplish a simple task. These strange machines, nicknamed RGMs, are excellent examples of chain reactions. A ball rolling down a ramp might set off toppling dominoes that might tip over a lever that turns on a blender that . . . You get the idea. Anyway, all these crazy machines were inspired by drawings by Rube Goldberg, an engineer who created cartoons that show the funny side of physics. If you're interested in making your own Rube Goldberg machine, here are some tips:

- Go on the Internet and watch videos of Rube Goldberg machines. You might get ideas for materials you can use. One of the master RGM builders is Joseph Herscher.

- Look around your house for odds and ends that might work well in a Rube Goldberg machine.

- Select a simple task for the machine to do.

- Play around with the materials to see how they might cause chain reactions in creative ways.

- Once you have a rough idea, test your machine over and over. Even the best RGM makers sometimes take hundreds of tries to get it to work just right!

••• EGG-SPERIMENT WITH INERTIA •••

· THE TRICK ·

Without touching an egg, make it splash down into a glass of water.

· PROPS ·

- metal pie pan
- 2 raw eggs (or more, in case some break during practice!)
- 2 cardboard toilet paper tubes
- 2 large drinking glasses
- water
- work space that can get messy and wet

· WHAT TO DO ·

1. Fill a glass halfway with water and center the pie pan on top of it.

2. Place a cardboard tube vertically on the pie pan, directly over the water glass.

3. Put one egg on top of the cardboard tube. Look at the setup from the side to make sure the egg and the tube are directly above the water.

4. Using one open hand, hit the pie pan horizontally and firmly with the inside of your fingers. Don't smack it so hard that the glass topples, though! The pan and tube will fly away, but the egg will drop down into the glass. This takes practice, so you may end up with a few broken eggs or spilled water. Keep trying until you get it right!

5. Once you get the knack of the simple version, try it with two eggs at once. Center the pie plate on two glasses, and when it is knocked away, the eggs will drop into the water. The setup for two eggs looks like this:

30

Jolly good! That stunt was exquisitely delightful and exceptionally awe-inspiring. I must tell you that when I first saw the egg, it brought back horrible memories of when I, the amazing Isaac Newton, had to work on a farm! My mother made *me* clean the chicken coop. It's true! She had no idea that I would one day become a brilliant scientist. But this "egg-speriment" also thrilled me, because it demonstrated *my* first law of motion. (Did my mother come up with any laws of motion? Of course not!) That's the one that says that moving things keep moving unless they are slowed down by an opposite force. It also says still things will stay still unless they are put in motion by an outside force. As my stalwart and sagacious colleague Einstein told you in the Penny in Orbit experiment, this phenomenon is called inertia.

So what does my first law of motion have to do with this experiment? The tube traveled with the pie plate when you hit it, but the egg—which was not touching the plate—was free to fall down into the water. Pulled down by our old friend gravity, of course! If you could see this all happening in slow motion, you'd see that the egg stayed "frozen" in the air for a fraction of a second while the plate flew to the side. This is because the opposite force of the cardboard tube was pushing upward, against gravity. Once the tube was gone, the force of gravity pulled the egg downward into the glass of water. The water, of course, cushioned the fall, so the egg didn't break.

CHAPTER 3

HOT AS FIRE, COLD AS ICE

When air is heated, its molecules move.
They bump and they bounce, which just goes to prove
They've gotten more energy, they're on the go.
They take up more space as they scatter and flow.
The stunts coming up are powered by heat.
So astound your friends with each physics feat!

Up, up, and awaayyyy! Nothing like a hot air balloon ride to get the blood pumping! Right, professors? Sir Newt, you're looking a little green! Try to relax, Alberto, this isn't a black hole. And Galiman, if you'd stop bird-watching I have something important to tell you. This is the chapter when we do some incredible tricks and stunts with fire, water, and ice.

Before we start, I have something SUPER IMPORTANT to tell you: The tricks and stunts in this chapter are very exciting and awesome—but you can't do them by yourself. When you are working with fire, you MUST have an Adult Sidekick with you so you don't get hurt.

· · TEA BAG ROCKET · · ·

· THE TRICK ·

In a flash, turn a tea bag into a rocket and launch it several feet in the air.

· PROPS ·

- tea bag (the paper kind with the string and tag)
- metal dish or nonflammable plate
- lighter or matches
- scissors
- two pairs of safety glasses
- safe work area (high ceiling, no draft from fans or air conditioners, no curtains nearby, etc.)
- Adult Sidekick

· WHAT TO DO ·

1. Cut the top off of the tea bag. Throw away the piece of bag, staple, string, and tag. Dump the tea in the trash.

2. Unfold the tea bag to form a rectangle, then gently roll it to form a cylinder and stand it up on the nonflammable plate.

3. Put on your safety glasses, and make sure your Adult Sidekick does, too. Then ask your Adult Sidekick to light the top of the tea bag.

4. Watch the flame travel down the tea bag rocket until it lifts in the air. Be sure the burning bag stays away from anything that could catch fire—including you! The rocket's flame will eventually burn itself out. When the remains land, make sure they are extinguished, then gently pick them up and toss them in the trash.

Gadzooks! Dr. Dazz's crazy hot air balloon ride was a vile, horrendous, and repugnant experience. In short, I hated it! I've never been one for heights. But hot air balloons did play an important role in the science of flight. Long before airplanes were invented, people flew through the air in hot air balloons. How do these marvelous vehicles work? These mighty balloons travel up because hot air rises over cold air. When you lit the rocket on fire, the air inside the tea bag cylinder heated up. This made the air molecules inside less dense than the cooler air around the rocket, so these heated molecules traveled upward. As this warm air moved, it pulled the remains of the tea bag with it, because the ash weighs so little.

FIRE IN SPACE

When you light a candle on Earth, the flame forms a teardrop shape. (Check out the flame under Einstein's hot dog.) This shape is formed when the gases around the flame heat up and rise upward. At the same time, gravity pulls colder air to the bottom of the flame. This feeds the flame fresh oxygen and keeps it burning. The yellow color of the candlelight comes from the wax melting into tiny particles of carbon called soot.

As these particles heat up in the flame, they glow bright yellow and rise up.

Thanks to experiments done on the International Space Station, we know that flames in space are a different shape and color. They are round and blue rather than teardrop-shaped and yellow. (Look at the flame under Astronaut Newton's hot dog.) Flames in space are different because there's so little gravity. In the microgravity of the space station, hot air expands but moves outward instead of upward. The flame forms a dome shape. Without gravity, soot doesn't burn, so the flame is blue, not yellow. In space, it is even possible for flames to curl into tiny balls and float around. One astronaut tweeted to Earth that such a sight looked like "a jellyfish of fire."

·· LEMON LIFTOFF ···

· THE TRICK ·

Use the powers of fire, water, and air pressure to levitate a slice of lemon.

· PROPS ·

- lemon slice, about ¼ inch thick
- 4 wooden matches
- nonflammable plate with a rim
- tall glass
- water
- Adult Sidekick

· WHAT TO DO ·

1. Place the slice of lemon in the middle of the plate.

2. Put three matches in a triangular pyramid on top of the lemon slice. The flammable match tips should all touch at the top.

3. Pour water into the plate until it is about ¼ inch deep, making the lemon slice float on top.

4. With help from your Adult Sidekick, light the fourth match and hold it under the tips of the match pyramid, lighting all three at about the same time.

5. Put the glass upside down over the lemon and matches.

6. Watch as the flame goes out and the water and lemon slice rise up in the glass!

The Science Behind the Stunt

Wunderbar! (That's German for *wonderful.*) The physics of this trick is a little tricky, so hang on and your Uncle Albert will get you through it. First, when you put a glass on top of the lit matches, the air inside the glass heats up. As the air gets hotter and hotter, the molecules move around more, expanding under the cup. It's like they're saying, "Let us outta here!"

Fire needs oxygen to keep burning, so when all the oxygen under the glass is used up, *POOF!* The matches go out, and the air inside the glass cools. The air molecules calm down and stop trying to escape. When the air shrinks down again, the water pushes up inside the glass to fill the space, and the lemon slice moves up because it is floating on the water! This proves my philosophy: When life gives you lemons, do an experiment!

• • • KETCH-UP, KETCH-DOWN • • •

• THE TRICK •

Make it look like the power of your mind can make a
ketchup packet float up and down in a bottle of water.

• PROPS •

- empty plastic water bottle with cap
- fast food ketchup packets (about 5)
- water
- bowl

· WHAT TO DO ·

1. Find a ketchup packet that will work for this trick. Not all ketchup packets have the same amount of air in them. You need to find a packet that floats on water. To test each packet, drop it in a bowl of water and see if it floats or sinks. As soon as you have a floater, go on to Step 2.

2. Put the ketchup packet into the empty plastic bottle, fill the bottle to the very top with water, and screw the cap on.

3. Hold the water bottle in one hand and gently squeeze and release it. As you do, the ketchup packet will go down as you squeeze and rise up as you release.

4. To make it look like you're controlling the ketchup packet with your mind, point at the packet with your other hand as you make the packet move up and down. If you add a look of great concentration as you do this, you can convince your audience that your powers of mind control are making the packet move! (The secret that you don't want your audience to see is that you're squeezing and releasing the bottle.) See if you can put just the right amount of pressure on the bottle to make the ketchup packet float in the middle.

The Science Behind the Stunt

By the moons of Jupiter, look what you've done! Bravo! You almost fooled me into thinking you moved that ketchup packet because of your mind. But I know better: Physics is the answer, not magic. The ketchup packet floats in the bottle of water because it contains a small amount of air, which is lighter than water. When you squeeze the bottle, the pressure forces the bubble of air inside the packet to condense into a smaller space. When you make the bubble smaller, you make the ketchup packet more dense, so it sinks. But when you release the bottle, the air bubble returns to its normal size, so the packet rises again. This classic experiment is sometimes called a Cartesian diver, named after René Descartes (1596–1650), a French scientist who did experiments with buoyancy. **Buoyancy** is the tendency of things to float or sink in water or air.

The physics behind this trick is similar to the way submarines work. Around the outside of a submarine are tanks. When these tanks are filled with water, the submarine sinks. But when air is forced into the tanks, the submarine rises to the surface.

··· CRUSH A CAN ···

· THE TRICK ·

You no longer need your hand to crush a soda can.
Use the power of air pressure to do it dramatically!

· PROPS ·

- empty soda can, rinsed out
- stove or hot plate
- tongs
- heat-resistant oven mitts
- large mixing bowl
- water
- ice
- Adult Sidekick

HOT PAD

1. Fill the bowl with ice and water.

2. Fill an empty soda can with about a tablespoon of water. IMPORTANT: Never heat a soda can when it is empty, as this could melt the can and be very dangerous.

3. Before you turn on the heat, put the soda can directly on a cool stove so it is stable. Put on your heat-resistant gloves and have your tongs ready.

4. Have your Adult Sidekick turn on the stove to heat up the water in the can for one minute. Look for steam to escape from the top of the soda can and listen for a bubbling sound.

5. After about a minute, use the tongs to carefully lift the soda can off the stove. Say some magic science words, such as "Alaka Zoorie Madame Curie!" then turn the can upside down into the bowl of water. *CRUNCH!* The can collapses.

The Science Behind the Stunt

Dazzling da Vinci! You must be flummoxed and flabbergasted. You're probably wondering: What caused the can to crush itself? Of course, I know the answer! After all, I *am* the incomparable Isaac Newton. The can was crushed because of a sudden change in air pressure. Let me explain. When you heated up the metal can, the air and the water inside it also became hotter and expanded. Some of the water became so hot, it turned into steam (gas) and escaped the can. This gas pushed out some of the air that was inside the can. When you flipped over the can into the icy water, the mouth of the can formed a seal against the surface of the water. When the icy water quickly cooled the expanded steam inside the can, it turned into a few drops of liquid. Since the air inside the can was no longer pushing outward on the metal with as much force, the air outside of the can had enough pressure to crush it. When an object collapses in on itself, scientists call it an **implosion**.

PHYSICS IN ACTION
How a Thermometer Works

Has your mama or papa ever taken your temperature when you were sick? Well, not to brag, but your old pal Galileo invented the first thermometer. In 1593, I was curious about how different materials respond to heat, so I invented a tool to measure changes in temperature. My thermometer looked very different from the type you use today.

So how does a modern thermometer measure changes in heat? The liquid inside a thermometer is usually made of colored alcohol. The tiny molecules that make up the liquid are always moving. When the alcohol is cooled by putting the thermometer in something cold, its molecules move slower and press closer together. This makes the liquid take up less space and slide down the glass tube. But when a thermometer is put in something warm, the alcohol molecules move faster and spread apart. This causes the alcohol to rise in the glass tube. Be careful: If the thermometer is heated too high, the alcohol molecules are forced to break through the glass!

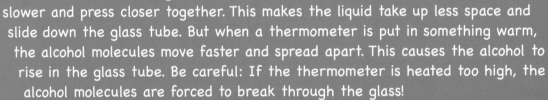

The numbers written on the thermometer help measure the specific temperatures. Scientists use different temperature scales for different purposes. The Fahrenheit scale was named after a German physicist named Gabriel D. Fahrenheit. On this scale, water freezes at 32 degrees and boils at 212 degrees. On the Celsius scale, named after a Swedish scientist named Anders Celsius, water freezes at zero degrees and boils at 100 degrees.

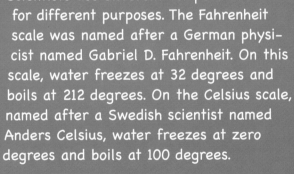

· · · INSTANT ICE · · ·

adult sidekick needed

· THE TRICK ·

Turn water to ice in a flash. How cool is that?

· PROPS ·

- 6 or more small bottles of purified water (in case one doesn't work)
- refrigerator
- freezer
- large metal container or bowl, tall enough for a water bottle to be submerged vertically

- small metal container or bowl
- clean thermometer
- ice cubes, crushed (about 4 to 6 cups)
- salt (any kind is okay)
- few ice cubes, *not* crushed
- Adult Sidekick

· WHAT TO DO ·

1. Refrigerate the bottles of water for at least one hour. At the same time, put the empty small metal bowl in the freezer.

2. Put one of the chilled water bottles in the tall metal container and surround it completely with a mix of crushed ice and salt. Wait about 15 to 20 minutes.

3. Carefully unscrew the top of the water bottle and stick the thermometer inside it. Your goal is to get the water to be about 15 to 20°F (-9 to -6°C). If the water is the right temperature, move to Step 4. Otherwise, remove the thermometer, screw on the cap, and keep it in the salt/ice mixture. Check it again every 5 to 10 minutes.

4. Remove the empty small metal bowl from the freezer and place an ice cube inside it.

5. Gently take the water bottle out of the icy salt water and slowly pour it onto the ice cube in the small bowl. The water will instantly freeze!

The Science Behind the Stunt

einstein

Stupendous! This stunt would have knocked my socks off—but I never wear socks. (I hate the things. Just call me Barefoot Al!) Let me explain the physics of this *wunderbar* trick. As you may know, water normally freezes when it gets to 32 degrees Fahrenheit (or 0 degrees Celsius). So why didn't the water in the bottle freeze when it dropped below that temperature? Ice crystals form fastest when they build on ice crystals that are already there or when there's some impurity to grow on, such as a tiny speck of dust. When ice crystals start to form, the process is called **nucleation**. Since the super cold water in this experiment is purified, it didn't have other ice or impurities to grow on, so the water stayed in liquid form longer than normal. But as soon as you poured the water on the ice cube, the nucleation process was jump-started and the water quickly turned into ice.

CHAPTER 4

THE MARVEL OF MAGNETS

> My magnetic suit has been attacked!
> Look at all the objects I did attract.
> I've got here a toaster, keys, and bowls . . .
> It's like I'm a magnet with north and south poles!

What can I say? I'm an attractive guy—especially when I'm wearing my magical, marvelous magnetic suit. Any metal that contains iron, nickel, or cobalt comes to me. Magnets are so useful. Sure, they hold pictures on the fridge, but they can do so much more! Machines called generators use magnets to create electricity. Magnets are used to make compass needles. Electromagnets in cranes help move big pieces of metal. In hospitals, X-ray and MRI machines use powerful magnets to get glimpses inside our bodies. Is it any wonder that *magic* and *magnet* start with the same three letters?

··· FLOATING DONUTS ···

· THE TRICK ·

Make round magnets float above one another on a pencil.

· PROPS ·

- unsharpened pencil
- 5 or more small O-shaped magnets, with holes big enough to fit the pencil through
- blob of modeling dough or clay
- table

· WHAT TO DO ·

1. Make the pencil stand up on a table by sticking the unsharpened writing end in a blob of modeling dough or clay.

2. Slide an O-shaped magnet on the unsharpened pencil so it slides to the bottom.

3. Take a second magnet and slide it over the top of the pencil. One of two things will happen: The two ring magnets will pull toward each other and stick, or they'll push apart. If the first situation happens, remove the second magnet, flip it over, and slide it back on the pencil so that they push apart.

4. Repeat Step 3 until all of the ring magnets are on the pencil and all but the first one is floating.

The Science Behind the Stunt

Magnets are marvelous! Or, as we say in Italian, *magneti sono meravigliosi!* Every magnet, no matter what its size or shape, has two poles: a north pole and a south pole. When the north pole of one magnet is put near the south pole of another magnet, they attract each other and stick together. In other words, opposite poles attract. But if two north poles (or two south poles) are put near each other, they push each other apart. In short, same poles repel each other. In this experiment, the magnets on the pencil look like they're floating because the two sides of each magnet facing each other are the same pole, so they push each other away.

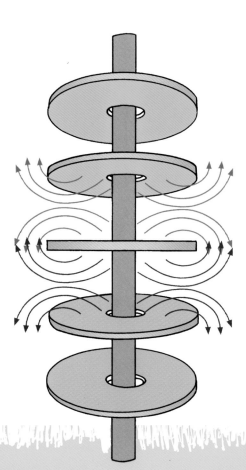

The invisible areas around a magnet are called **magnetic fields**. These fields are where their pulling/pushing effects can be felt. The farther away from the magnet you go, the weaker the magnet's pulling or pushing power. If you could see the magnetic fields around the magnets in this experiment, they would look like this. I hope you understand why this trick works. Ciao!

GIVE MY MAGNET LIFE! · · ·

· THE TRICK ·

Turn an ordinary nail—presto!—into a magnet that can be turned on and off.

· PROPS ·

- new D cell battery
- large iron nail (at least 3 inches long)
- insulated copper wire (2 to 3 feet)
- pliers to cut wire
- electrical tape
- pile of paper clips
- Adult Sidekick

· WHAT TO DO ·

1. Touch the end of the large nail to the pile of paper clips, then lift up the nail. Not surprisingly, the clips just sit there.

2. With the help of your Adult Sidekick, remove about an inch of plastic coating from each end of the wire. Wrap the insulated copper wire tightly around most of the nail, leaving 8 inches of loose wire on both ends. Don't let the wire overlap itself as you wrap it.

3. Use tape to attach the ends of the wire to the positive and negative ends of the battery. Touch the nail to the pile of paper clips again. Now you have an electromagnet that lifts them up! WARNING: If you leave the wires connected to the battery for a long time, they can become hot.

4. Have fun experimenting. Find out how strong your magnet is by seeing how many paper clips you can lift at once. Does your homemade electromagnet work if you only have one of the ends of the wire attached to the battery? See what happens if you repeat this experiment just using the coiled wire (without the nail inside it). How do these changes affect the electromagnet's power?

5. When you're done, remove the wires from the battery.

You did it! *Glückwünsche!* That's German for *congratulations*. You made your very own electromagnet. Magnets like the ones in the Floating Donuts experiment are magnetic all the time, so they are called **permanent magnets**. They create their own magnetic fields. The nail in this experiment doesn't become magnetic until you create a magnetic field around it using the battery's electricity. The electromagnet you created is called a temporary magnet. **Temporary magnets** are only magnetic as long as something creates a magnetic field for them—either a source of electricity or a permanent magnet. Just like a permanent magnet, your temporary electromagnet has north and south poles that can attract or repel, depending on what magnetic forces are near them.

How are electricity and magnetism related? In other words, how in the world does electricity from the battery turn the wire and nail into a magnet? The answer has to do with the itty-bitty parts that make up everything: **atoms**. Atoms are so small, you can't even see them with a microscope. They have even smaller parts called **electrons** whizzing around their edges. Electrons act like tiny magnets, with north and south poles of their own. *Before* you activated your electromagnet by connecting the wires to the battery, all these electrons were facing in different directions, so the wire and nail didn't have a charge. But *after* you turned on the electromagnet by connecting it to the battery, the electrons flowed from the battery through the wire near the nail and lined up like soldiers. This caused all the north poles of the electrons to point one way and the south poles to point the other. That means they all worked together like the electrons of a permanent magnet. When you removed the wire from the battery, the electrons returned to their random positions. What makes the wire get hot? The wire heats up because of the friction caused by the electrons pushing their way through it.

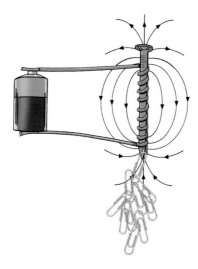

THE DISCOVERY OF ELECTROMAGNETISM

The discovery of electromagnetism is considered one of the most important scientific discoveries ever. Electromagnets are essential to many modern machines and tools, including doorbells, rock concert speakers, generators, cars, and airplanes. In fact, anything that uses an electric motor is probably powered, at least in part, by electromagnets.

The connection between magnetism and electricity was unknown until 1820, when a Danish scientist named Hans Ørstead observed something weird: Whenever he put a wire near a compass and ran electricity through the wire, the compass needle (a magnet) would wiggle. He knew something curious was going on, but he couldn't figure out the physics behind his discovery. What did electricity have to do with magnetism?

Many scientists tried to solve the mystery. Then a French physicist and mathematician named André-Marie Ampère made some discoveries. He experimented with two wires, each of which was carrying an electric current. He found that the direction that the electricity was flowing through the wire mattered. If both wires had their currents going in the same direction, the wires would be attracted (like magnets). But when the wires had currents going in opposite directions, the wires would repel each other, or push each other apart. In other words, the moving electrons in the wire created a magnetic field.

In 1831, a British scientist named Michael Faraday (one of Einstein's heroes) also made some discoveries about electromagnetism. He knew that when an electric current runs through a wire, it creates a magnetic field around the wire. Faraday's big brainstorm happened when he wondered, *What if the opposite were true? What if a magnetic field could create an electric current on a wire?* To find out, he moved a magnet through a coil of wire, then observed what happened. Yes! The moving magnet produced an electric current. He also figured out that the direction the magnet moves affects which direction the current will flow. When he moved the magnet quickly through the wire, it created a stronger current. When he coiled the wire, it increased the magnetic field that was produced when electricity was run through it.

Michael Faraday

TRAINS IN THE AIR

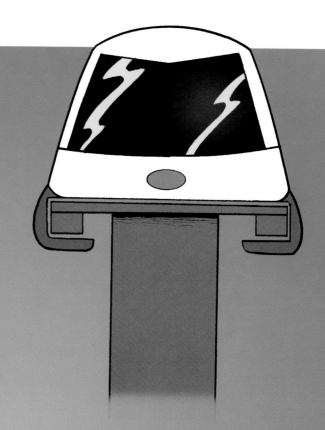

It sounds like something out of Harry Potter's world: trains that float above the tracks. But engineers have used physics to create Maglev trains, short for "magnetically levitated." Rather than riding on traditional train tracks, using the science of magnetic poles, Maglev trains float about an inch over special guideways. To lift a huge train takes some serious magnet power! They use superstrong electromagnets made from superconductive metals, which create magnetic fields that are much stronger than traditional magnets.

The superstrong magnets allow Maglev trains to race along at mind-blowing speeds, because there is no friction between the trains and the tracks below them. According to Guinness World Records, a Maglev train in Japan went over 360 miles per hour in 2003. (Most normal trains go about 100 to 200 miles per hour!) Scientists believe that these kinds of trains have the potential to go much faster. But safety always comes first, so scientists continue to do many tests before letting paying passengers ride the newest trains.

· · · COMPASS TREASURE HUNT · · ·

· THE TRICK ·

Make a homemade compass, then challenge
a friend to use it to find a hidden treasure.

· PROPS ·

- sewing needle or straightened paper clip
- pin or small nail (for testing if needle is magnetized)
- magnet (preferably with north and south poles labeled)
- red permanent marker
- shallow bowl filled with about 1 inch of water
- something light, round, and about an inch across that floats, such as a piece of cork, the plastic cap from a milk bottle, or the bottom of a paper cup
- a non-windy space
- a friend

· WHAT TO DO ·

1. Turn the sewing needle or straightened paper clip into a magnet by rubbing one end of it with the north pole of your magnet about thirty times. Rub the magnet in only one direction: Each time you get to the end of the needle, lift the magnet and move it away from the needle before rubbing again. Test if the needle is magnetized by seeing if it can pick up the pin or small nail.

2. Color the magnetized end of the needle red with the permanent marker.

3. Float the cork circle (or whatever floating material you use) on the water in the dish and gently place the needle on it. Make sure there is no wind. The needle

should point north. Use a professional compass (or a compass app on a computerized device) to check if your homemade compass points in the right direction. The magnetism in your compass will last for a couple hours, then will need to be remagnetized.

4. Hide a prize in your house or yard (as long as it isn't too windy!) and create a simple treasure map using compass points. Then have a friend use your homemade compass to find it. Have them place the compass on the ground so it is steady. Clues could say things like, "Walk 5 feet north, then walk 2 feet to the west," and so on.

The Science Behind the Stunt

Wunderbar! Let Uncle Albert tell you a little story. When I was just five years old growing up in Germany, I was sick in bed. I was so *schrecklich* that I felt like *erbrechen* my guts out. To cheer me up, my papa gave me a compass. I was so excited, I thought I would *plotz*! I was thrilled to learn that the needle was controlled by an invisible force—Earth's magnetic field.

So what's the science behind your homemade compass? Every time you rubbed the permanent magnet on the steel needle, you rubbed some magnetic stuff onto it and turned it into a temporary magnet. What makes your compass's needle always point north? Earth is a huge magnet, surrounded by a magnetic field. Deep in the center of the Earth there are magnetic materials, such as nickel and iron, that are constantly rolling around. These make our planet produce weak magnetic fields. Because of this, any *unattached* magnetic objects—like a needle floating on water—will line up with the poles so that one end faces north.

Here's something wild to think about: The metals deep inside the Earth's core are always moving, so our planet's magnetic fields never stay in the exact same locations. In fact, a million years ago, the North Pole is where the South Pole is now!

THE FIRST COMPASSES

You might think that I, the incomparable Isaac Newton, invented the first compass. While I did make many famous and important discoveries, the first compass was not one of them. Hundreds of years before I was born, clever inventors in China created the first compasses. They weren't used to help people navigate in the woods or at sea. No, sirree! These early compasses were used to create order and harmony in a home. Today, this design idea is called feng shui (pronounced "fung shway").

The first compasses were made by placing a spoon-shaped piece of a metal called a lodestone on a bronze square so it could turn in any direction. Other early compasses resembled the one you just made. The user floated a thin piece of wood in the shape of a fish in a bowl of water. This fish contained a magnetized needle, so it would point north.

CHAPTER 5

THE SOUNDS OF SCIENCE

Check out these instruments! Hear these strange sounds!
My musical talent knows no bounds.
These notes aren't caused by prestidigitation*.
No, they are due to the science of vibration!
If you could see sound as it flew through the air,
You'd see cool wavy lines going from here to there.

*fancy word for magic

I know what you're thinking: How can one guy be *sooo* talented? Honestly, sometimes I even surprise myself!

Now it's time for you to make some marvelous music of your own using the power of science! Try this: Hold your hand on your throat and hum. Then sing the words, "Let's make music!" Feel the vibrations? When you sing or talk, your vocal cords shake back and forth as you breathe out, which sends out vibrations. In this chapter, you're going to turn some ordinary objects—like straws, wineglasses, and coat hangers—into musical instruments. The key to unlocking their sounds is to learn how to make them vibrate, or shake back and forth, like you felt in your throat when you hummed and sang. (As an added bonus, some of these sounds are so obnoxious that they'll drive the nearest adults bananas!)

••• STRAW SYMPHONY •••

• THE TRICK •

Make a straw oboe and perform a cacophony of crazy sounds.

• PROPS •

- plastic straws (not the bendy kind)
- scissors

• WHAT TO DO •

CUT #1   CUT #2

1. Bite the end of a straw to flatten it, about ¾ inch from the end. The flatter, the better.

2. Make a diagonal cut across the flattened end of the straw.

3. Make another diagonal cut going the opposite way, so you end up with a triangular tip on the top of the straw. The bases of the two cuts should be even with each other.

4. Stick this flattened triangular tip into your mouth and blow through it. Do you hear a buzzing sound? Keep trying until you hear it. You might need to slide the straw forward or backward in your mouth to find just the right place. You also might need to experiment with how hard you blow or how flattened the straw is.

5. Once you master the basic buzz, the real fun begins! As you blow on your straw and make the buzzing sound, cut the other end of the straw a bit at a time. You'll hear the pitch of your sound get higher and higher.

THE ALL-STRAW JAZZ BAND

GALILEO

When I was a boy, my papa and I loved to make music together at home. I would spend hours experimenting with different string instruments to see how they worked. In my books, I wrote about how sound travels in waves through the air, kind of the way a pebble creates ripples in a pond. These waves reach your ears and send signals to your brain.

When you blow in the flattened part of the straw, the two pieces of the tip vibrate together. These vibrations travel down the straw and bounce around inside it, which causes the air molecules nearby to move around. This movement creates sound waves that travel through the air to your ears. The sound is made louder by the tube shape of the straw, because the rounded inside gives the sound waves lots of places to bounce around. When you cut the straw shorter and shorter, the pitch (highness or lowness) gets higher because the same number of sound waves bounce around in less space. The way this straw instrument makes music is similar to how most reed instruments, like clarinets and oboes, work.

··· SPOOKY SOUNDS ···

· THE TRICK ·

Use your finger to make a wineglass produce a haunting sound.

· PROPS ·

- wineglass (the thinner the glass, the better)
- cup of water
- Adult Sidekick

· WHAT TO DO ·

1. Hold down the bottom of a wineglass and gently flick the top rim with your pointer finger so it "pings." Does it make a sound? If so, count how long it lasts. For this trick to work well, you want a wineglass that "pings" for at least three seconds. The longer the "ping," the better the music you'll be able to create.

2. Fill the wineglass halfway with water. Have your Adult Sidekick hold the base of the glass while you wet your finger and press it gently on the rim, then move your finger around the rim. Keep moving your finger continuously in a circle. Be careful not to press too hard or you'll break the glass. Eventually you'll hear a sound. This can take practice to get it right, so don't be discouraged if your glass doesn't sing right away.

3. Add more water to the glass, have your Adult Sidekick hold it down, then rub your finger around the rim again. How did the pitch change—was the sound higher or lower? What do you predict will happen if you add even more water? Find out!

4. Fill the glass almost to the top and rub your finger around the rim. Look carefully at the water as you move your finger. You should be able to see tiny vibrations on the surface.

Try this: Gently flick an empty wineglass so it vibrates, then put your hands around the bowl part of the glass. The sound will stop. Why do you think this happens?

Jolly good show, my inquisitive apprentice! Why did we use wineglasses for this experiment? Wineglasses are made of thin glass, so they vibrate easily when hit or touched in a certain way. Remember one of my famous laws of motion: For every action, there is a reaction. When you "ping" the glass with your finger (action), the glass responds by making a sound (reaction). That's because the glass is vibrating back and forth *hundreds* of times per second. All these tiny movements create sound waves. And when you rub your wet finger around the top of the glass, it sticks then slides, sticks then slides. Your fingers are not smooth; they have little ridges on them (which make up your finger print). When these ridges are moistened and rubbed along the edge of the glass, the friction of the sticking and sliding makes the glass vibrate, which sends sound waves traveling through the air to your ears. The bowl shape of the wineglass helps, too. It amplifies the sound (makes it louder) because it gives the vibrations lots of places to bounce back and forth. Of course, if you hold the bowl of the glass while you rub, you won't hear any spooky sounds, because your holding it is preventing the vibration.

NEWTON

WINEGLASS CONCERT

If you line up eight wineglasses with increasing amounts of water, it's possible to play a musical scale. And some people take it even further! To see some remarkable examples of people playing famous music with a bunch of wineglasses, go online and search for "wineglass symphony" or "Für Elise on glass harp" and you'll be treated to wild versions of the experiment you just did.

··· SECRET BELLS ···

· THE TRICK ·

Discover chimes hidden in a coat hanger.

· PROPS ·

- metal coat hanger
- string or yarn (about 6 feet)
- scissors

· WHAT TO DO ·

1. Hit the coat hanger against a table and listen to the sound it makes. How would you describe it? Now get ready to reveal some hidden sounds!

2. Cut two pieces of string, each about 3 feet long, and tie each one near the corner of the coat hanger.

3. Twirl each of the unattached ends of the string around your pointer fingers. Leave the tips of your fingers exposed when you wrap the string around them. There should be at least 12 inches of loose string between your fingers and the coat hanger.

4. Place both your pointer fingers (with the strings around them) in your ears, then gently swing the hanger against a wall or chair. How would you describe the sound the hanger makes in your ears?

5. Experiment with different lengths of string between your ears and the hanger. You can also attach other objects, such as a metal spoon, to the string to see if you can discover any more secret sounds.

Glückwünsche, you did it! When I put the strings in my ears, I didn't expect much, then *überraschung*! I had a big surprise. What's going on? How come the hanger sound is so short and high-pitched when you just bang it on the table, but when you put the little strings on it and stick your fingers in your ears as you bang it—WOW! It sounds like chimes, or church bells!

As you probably figured out, it's all about vibrations. In the first case, the hanger's vibrations don't last very long because they are stopped by your hand. But when the hanger is attached to the strings, it can vibrate long after it hits the wall. The vibrations travel up the strings and go directly into your ears, which take the sound signals to your brain. The sound is louder when your fingers are near your ears because the vibrations travel better through the tight string threads and your hands than through the air.

Uncle Albert has another story for you. My *mutter* loved to play piano, so there was always music around my house. When I was six, my parents made me take violin lessons. At first, I didn't like them very much, but then when I was thirteen, I fell in love with Mozart's music. When I play his sonatas, my heart *schlägt mit Freude*—that's German for "beats with joy."

AMAZING EARS

You may have heard that dogs have an excellent sense of hearing and can pick up sounds we can't. Why is that? Sound is caused by vibrations in the air. The more vibrations, the higher the sound. Humans cannot hear sounds that vibrate at more than twenty thousand vibrations per second, but dogs can hear up to fifty thousand vibrations per second.

Not only can dogs hear higher-pitched sounds than we can, they also hear sounds about four times farther away. If you can hear something twenty feet away, a dog can hear it eighty feet away! But dogs are hardly the top hearers in the animal kingdom. Even cats have a better sense of hearing than dogs.

Bats use their super hearing and a technique called echolocation to catch flying insects. It's similar to the Marco Polo game kids play in the pool. You know, the one in which you close your eyes and call out "Marco!" and the people you are chasing call out "Polo!" So, by following the sounds, you find your "prey." Some kinds of moth, a bat's favorite prey, have evolved the ability to detect the sounds that bats send out to catch them. The tiger moth not only can hear a bat's clicks, it can imitate the clicks and send them back at a rate of 450 clicks per tenth of a second! This, of course, confuses the bat.

DEAF MUSICIANS ROCK OUT

You might think that if someone is deaf or has other serious hearing difficulties, they couldn't enjoy a rock concert. Not true! Just because someone can't hear the melodies and lyrics doesn't mean they can't enjoy the exciting vibrations of some of the instruments. When a bass guitar is played, or a drum solo blasts through the speakers, many hearing-impaired rock fans have a wonderful time. Many rock concerts now have special ASL (American Sign Language) performers who help capture the song's energy and message and translate it for those who cannot hear.

Even cooler: The idea of deaf musicians might seem impossible, but a rock group called Beethoven's Nightmare proves it can work. This group name was inspired by Ludwig van Beethoven, a classical composer who famously went deaf at thirty-five—but then went on to write stunning music. This band is made up of three guys—Bob Hiltermann, Ed Chevy, and Steve Longo—who all grew up deaf. As kids, they watched their hearing friends listen to rock music, so they put on headphones, cranked up the volume super loud, and enjoyed the vibrations. They met one another at Gallaudet University, a school for the deaf and hard of hearing in Washington, DC. There, they realized they shared a passion for rock 'n' roll, so they formed a band. They graduated and went their separate ways, but years later, they got together for a reunion and decided to form a new band. Before every show, they hand out balloons to their audiences, so hearing and deaf fans can feel the vibrations that blast from the huge speakers behind the performers.

CHAPTER 6

THE COLOR OF LIGHT

Do you know why a rainbow never ends?
Or how it makes colors when sunlight bends?
You'll find out the answers and make a rainbow for keeps.
But first it's time to spray my peeps!

WHAT RAINBOW???

Have you ever made a rainbow like this? I love rainbows, not only because they're beautiful, but also because they spark some interesting questions: What causes rainbows? Why are they always curved? Why do the colors always show up in the same order? Why can't my team of phenomenal physicists see my rainbow from where they're standing?

COOL FACTS ABOUT RAINBOWS

- Rainbows are only visible if the sun is behind you. For this reason, you can never view a rainbow from its side. In this picture, Newton, Galileo, and Einstein can't see Dr. Dazz's rainbow.

- Rainbows are not flat. That's just an optical illusion. The water droplets that make rainbows are a three-dimensional cloud.

- The colors of the rainbow are caused when the sun's white light bends, or **refracts**, in the water droplets. The colors bend at slightly different angles as they travel through the mist. Think of white light as skateboarders hitting a ramp: Some colors of light can jump a little higher on the ramp than others, with red jumping the highest and blue jumping the lowest.

- Sometimes we see double rainbows. A second, fainter rainbow forms the same way as the main rainbow, but the light is reflected twice. Because of this double reflection, the light leaves the raindrops at a different angle, so it appears higher. What's weird about this second rainbow is that the colors are in the opposite order.

A RAINBOW FOR KEEPS

Create a long-lasting rainbow that you can put on your bedroom wall.

· PROPS ·

- shallow pan made of foil or glass (medium size)
- black construction paper
- scissors
- pitcher or large cup
- water
- clear nail polish
- paper towels

· WHAT TO DO ·

1. Cut the black construction paper so it fits inside the pan.

2. Use the pitcher or cup to fill the pan with about one to two inches of water. Use your fingers to press the paper below the surface. Eventually the water will weigh it down.

3. Carefully put **one drop** of nail polish on top of the water in the pan. Wait ten to thirty seconds as you watch the nail polish spread out. Voilà, a rainbow!

4. Wait five minutes for the nail polish to dry.

5. While you wait, lay out paper towels on a flat surface where you can set the black paper to dry.

6. Pick up the black paper by the corners and slowly lift it so the nail polish rainbow sits atop it. As the paper touches the rainbow, the nail polish will stick to it. Transfer the black paper to the paper towels to dry.

7. Once the paper and nail polish are dry, hold the paper flat toward the light and view it at a low angle. You should see a swirl of colors!

Sensational! I, the remarkable Isaac Newton, am deeply fascinated by the science of light, known as optics. I'm the chap who discovered that white light is made up of all the colors of the rainbow! To understand this experiment, you have to know that light travels at different speeds depending on what it is traveling through. When light moves through the air, it travels at about 186,000 miles (300,000 kilometers) per second. But it travels about a third slower when it moves through water, and even slower as it goes through nail polish. When light is slowed down as it passes through water or nail polish, it bends, or refracts.

As I mentioned, white light is made up of all the other colors of the rainbow. Sounds bizarre, huh? Each color has a different wavelength and travels at a different speed. When light hits the nail polish, the various colors slow down at different speeds as they refract through the liquid, which creates the rainbow effect. The colors you see are also affected by the thickness of the polish—it's thicker in the middle than at the edges, so there's more polish to slow down the light waves and a farther distance to travel.

In 1665, I, the great Sir Isaac Newton, did some what you would call "wicked cool" experiments with light. In my brilliant book *Opticks*, I shared my discoveries about how light works. In one famous experiment, I put a triangular piece of glass called a **prism** in the path of a ray of sunlight, and I found that the prism separated the sunlight into a rainbow of colors. I called the pattern of colors in a rainbow a **spectrum**. These colors always appear in the same order: red, orange, yellow, green, blue, indigo, and violet. Each color in the spectrum is caused by light bending at a different angle. After I used the first prism to separate the light into a rainbow, I then put a second prism upside down on the other side of the refracted colors. This prism put all the colors back together again into white light! The nail polish in this experiment acted as a prism, bending the light into a permanent rainbow.

••• LASER LIGHT BEND-O-RAMA •••

adult sidekick needed

· THE TRICK ·

Light normally travels in a straight line—but you can bend it!

· PROPS ·

- laser pointer
- clear and empty 1-liter plastic soda bottle with cap
- nail
- water
- kitchen sink or deep pan
- masking tape or duct tape
- dimly lit room
- spray bottle with mist setting (optional)
- Adult Sidekick

· WHAT TO DO ·

1. Prepare the soda bottle by using a nail to poke a small hole in the side of it, about 3 inches from the bottom.

2. Cover the hole with your finger and fill the bottle all the way to the top with water, then screw on the cap. Stand the bottle upright and slowly remove your finger. Why doesn't the water come out the hole?

3. Now stand the bottle in a sink or deep pan and unscrew the top. Why did the water start to flow? After a few seconds, screw the cap back on. Put a piece of duct or masking tape over the hole.

4. Time to explore your laser with some assistance from your Adult Sidekick! Shine the laser pointer on a wall. If you wish, turn off the lights and spray the laser's path with some water from a spray bottle. You'll see the beam of light as it travels straight across the room. (IMPORTANT: Never shine the laser in anyone's eyes, as this could cause injury.)

5. Point the laser so it shines through the soda bottle to the hole on the other side. Peel back the tape and let the light shine through the hole. Unscrew the cap and let the water escape in an arc. Look what happens to the laser light!

64

Wunderbar! This delightful experiment raises two intriguing questions that Uncle Albert will try to answer. First, why didn't the water leak out the hole when the cap was on? The water molecules near the hole pressed together and closed it off. This kind of seal is called **surface tension**. When you unscrewed the cap, more air got into the bottle and created pressure to push down on the water from above. This air pressure broke the surface tension, making the water go *zooooop* out the little hole. Good old gravity pulled on the stream of water, giving it an arc shape.

Second, why did the laser light bend with the escaping stream of water? The answer is the light got trapped inside the stream. When a beam of light gets trapped and bounces around in a stream of water or glass tube, scientists call it **total internal reflection**. As light moves from the more dense water to the less dense air, it refracts, or bends. The light also bounces around, or reflects, inside the water stream. It becomes "stuck" in the water and can't escape into the air. This physics idea is how fiber optic cables work. These cables are superthin glass that carry digital information over long distances. They work by turning sound waves into patterns of light that bounce inside the glass lines, just like the laser bounces in the stream of water in this experiment.

THE SPEED OF LIGHT

Four hundred years ago, most scientists thought that light traveled instantly. But not me! I had a hunch they were wrong, so I did an experiment to see how fast light travels. One night in 1600, my assistant and I went to hills in Italy that were one mile apart and each held lanterns with covers on them. We flashed these lights at each other and tried to measure how long it took for the light to travel. And you know what we found out? We discovered that light travels much too fast to be measured that way. But I didn't give up and kept asking smart questions about how light travels.

Today we know that light travels at about 186,000 miles per second. At this speed, it takes the sun's light about eight minutes to reach us. So if the sun suddenly disappeared, we on Earth wouldn't know it for eight minutes. When you look at the stars at night, you're actually seeing the light that left those stars long ago. The closest star to us (other than the sun) is Proxima Centauri. Since its distance is four light-years away, this means the light that you see when you look at this star actually left the star four years ago!

· · · COIN? WHAT COIN? · · ·

· THE TRICK ·

Make a coin vanish from under a glass!

· PROPS ·

- clear drinking glass
- saucer or round piece of cardboard
- pitcher of water
- coin

· WHAT TO DO ·

1. Put the bottom of the drinking glass on top of the coin and place the saucer on top of the glass. Look at the coin through the side of the glass. It's still there, right?

2. Remove the saucer and use the pitcher to fill the glass with water. As you do this, watch the glass from the side. Say some goofy magic science words, like, "Who needs distraction when you have refraction?!" Replace the saucer, then look at the bottom of the glass. Where did the coin go?

3. When you're ready to have the coin reappear, say some other silly magic words, such as, "Zippity zing! Zippity zoing! Use science to bring back the coin!" then lift the glass and the coin will be visible again.

The Science Behind the Stunt

By the whiskers of my bushy beard, that was *molto magico*! Of course, the real reason the coin seemed to disappear can be explained by physics. As you probably guessed, the coin never actually left the bottom of the glass. So why were your eyes fooled when you poured the water on it? The answer has to do with the fact that light bends when it travels through water. Normally, when light rays travel through the air, there is no refraction—it doesn't bend. But when water is poured into the glass, both the water and the glass cause the light to refract. For an object to be visible, light has to bounce off it and enter our eyes. But in this experiment, none of the light hitting the coin bounces and hits our eyes from the angle at which you look into the glass; it bends in another direction. Since our brains usually think that light from objects travels in a straight line, we are fooled into thinking the coin has disappeared.

CHAPTER 7

ELECTRO-WOW!

Our time together's almost done! This chapter is the last.
I know this may sound SHOCKING, but please don't be aghast.
The power of these magic tricks comes from electricity.
The power of my snazzy clothes? That's just eccentricity!

To understand what causes electricity, you need to learn about atoms. Everything is made of super itty-bitty things called atoms. How small are they? A clever chemistry teacher named Jonathan Bergmann explains that atoms are so small that if each of the atoms in *one* grapefruit were blown up to the size of a blueberry, the enlarged grapefruit would take up as much space as the Earth!

Atoms are made up of three parts: protons, neutrons, and electrons. The protons and neutrons are found in the center of the atom in an area called the **nucleus**, and a cloud of electrons whiz around the outside of the nucleus. Electrons can move from one atom to another. This movement of electrons is what causes electricity.

The parts of an atom have different electrical charges. Protons have a positive charge, electrons have a negative charge, and neutrons have no charge. Before I rubbed my shoes on this carpet, they had no charge, because they had the same number of protons and electrons. But when I rubbed them, they picked up some electrons from the carpet and became negatively charged. And when I touch Sir Newt, those electrons will jump from my body to his—*zap!*

···MIND-CONTROL STRAW···

· THE TRICK ·

Use the power of your mind to make a straw twirl!
Or at least make it *look* like that!

· PROPS ·

- drinking straw in a paper wrapper
- unopened water bottle

· WHAT TO DO ·

1. Take a wrapped straw and tear off the end of the paper wrapper. Then pinch the uncovered end of the straw firmly with your thumb and pointer finger and quickly pull off the wrapper. This will "charge up" your straw. You can also charge up a straw by rubbing it on a shirt or a paper napkin.

2. Touching the straw as little as possible (you don't want to lose the charge!), carefully balance it across the cap of the unopened water bottle. This can be tricky, because the straw is attracted to your fingers.

3. Move the fingers of one hand near the end of the straw, but don't actually touch it. The straw will move on its own, attracted to your fingers. Then move your fingers near the other end of the straw and it will move in the other direction. If this doesn't work at first, you may wish to try a different type of straw (thicker straws tend to work better). You can recharge a straw by rubbing it against a shirt or inside a folded piece of paper.

4. When you're done moving the straw "with your mind," touch the straw to discharge it and give it to a friend to try. It will not move when they put their hands near it (unless they charge it up again).

The Science Behind the Stunt

Aha! The mind is indeed a powerful thing. Here's another true story: When I was growing up, I loved riding my bicycle. One day, I watched the rays of sunlight and wondered, *What would it be like to ride on a beam of light?* It was one of my first thought experiments.

Now, let's talk about the science of the straw trick. As you might have guessed, the secret to moving the straw has *nothing* to do with mind control and *everything* to do with static electricity. Static electricity is the buildup of an electrical charge on the surface of an object. (*Static* means non-moving; the charge sticks there and is not flowing.) If you put a statically charged object near an object called a conductor, the charge can be released, or it can cause the two objects to be attracted to each other.

When you rubbed the straw on the straw paper (or shirt), you pulled off billions of tiny, invisible electrons from the paper and added them to the straw. Electrons have a negative charge. Some materials, like plastic, glass, and cloth, hold on to their electrons very tightly. Such materials are called **insulators**. Other materials called **conductors** let go of their electrons more easily. Metals are often good conductors. In this stunt, when you put the negatively charged straw near your fingers, it is attracted because fingers are good conductors. That's because atoms with an opposite charge are attracted to each other.

This trick might work better some days than others. If it's humid out, all the moisture in the air can remove your fingers' charge. But if you do the trick right after walking on a thick rug with plastic-soled shoes while wearing a sweater, you will be very positively charged and it will work very well!

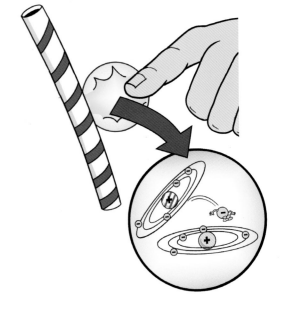

··· ROLLING CANS, JUMPING CEREAL ···

· THE TRICK ·

Make a soda can roll without touching it.
Then make crispy rice cereal jump in the air!

· PROPS ·

- empty soda can
- 2 or more balloons
- crispy rice cereal
- head of hair (the hairier, the better!)

· WHAT TO DO ·

1. Put the soda can on its side on a flat surface, such as a table or floor.

2. Blow up the balloon and tie it. Then rub it quickly back and forth in your hair.

3. Move the balloon close to the can without touching it. The can will move toward the balloon. You can put the balloon on the other side of the can, and it will attract the can in the other direction.

4. Put a handful of crispy rice cereal on the table, then rub the balloon again on your hair. Hold the balloon over the cereal and watch it leap into the air.

Try this: Give your friend a second can and balloon and have a race to see who can use the magic of static electricity to pull their can faster from point A to point B.

The Science Behind the Stunt

If someone says the straw moves by magic, you tell them your sagacious and erudite pal Isaac Newton said, "Poppycock!" The force that makes the straw move is once again static electricity. When you rub the balloon in your hair, you're pulling negatively charged electrons from your hair and transferring them onto the balloon. The negatively charged balloon pulls against the soda can, causing it to move toward it. Similarly, the negatively charged balloon causes any small object with a neutral or positive charge to move toward it. That's why the crispy cereal leaps up.

WEIRD ENERGY

You probably know that wind and water can generate power by converting mechanical energy into electricity. And you've no doubt heard that the sun's energy can be transformed into electricity by using solar panels. But some creative thinkers have explored even stranger ways to make energy.

Four clever teenage girls in Nigeria created a generator that is powered by urine. This pee-powered machine removed the hydrogen from urine and powered their generator for several hours. It didn't create a lot of electricity, but it is an intriguing idea.

A large onion factory in California has found a new solution for all the waste they toss: Turning it into electricity. They were creating over 1.5 million pounds of onion trimmings a week that was just spread as fertilizer on their fields. They hired some scientists to help them figure out how to turn this onion waste into hydrogen gas and the gas into electricity!

> I can't believe we've reached the end!
> It's time for us to go.
> I hope you had some physics fun.
> Now put on your own show!

FAREWELL, MY FRIENDS!

Holy Einstein's eyebrows! Is this really the end of the book? I had hoped it would go on forever like a laser beam. Well, I hope you had a blast performing some amazing science stunts for your friends and family. Before we go, I must thank the talented trio who helped explain the physics behind these tricks. Give it up for my brilliant pals Galileo, Newton, and Einstein!

THE REAL GALILEO, NEWTON, AND EINSTEIN

Dr. Dazz exists only in this book, but the cartoon versions of Galileo, Isaac Newton, and Albert Einstein are based on real science superstars. I included many true details about their remarkable lives, but exaggerated their personalities for the sake of humor. I encourage you to read their biographies to learn how these geniuses followed their curiosity and overcame obstacles. Here's a glimpse of what these guys were really like.

GALILEO GALILEI (1564–1642)

Known as the Father of Modern Science, Galileo was fascinated by the night sky. About four hundred years ago in Italy, he made homemade telescopes. (He didn't invent the first telescope, but his versions were much more powerful than those before them.) Using them, he discovered that the moon has mountains, Jupiter has moons, and Venus goes through phases. At a time when many people believed that the sun orbited the Earth, Galileo wrote a book that said the opposite was true—and mocked people for thinking otherwise! This got him in big trouble with the Catholic Church. Galileo was put on trial, forced to say his ideas were wrong, and wasn't allowed to leave his house. In 1992, the Catholic Church apologized for their treatment of Galileo three hundred and fifty years after his death.

Weird But True . . .

- Ninety-five years after Galileo died, his body was dug up and moved. Before he was buried again, an admirer cut off the middle finger of his right hand. This finger is now in a glass egg at the Museo Galileo in Florence, Italy. (Look online for "Galileo's finger" if you dare!)

SIR ISAAC NEWTON (1642–1727)

The year Galileo died, Newton was born in England. His mother wanted him to work on their family farm, but Newton hated farming. He did, however, love science and math. Fortunately, his uncle and schoolmaster spotted his genius and helped him get into the University of Cambridge. There, he made many discoveries. By experimenting with prisms, he figured out that white light contains all the colors of the rainbow. Based on Galileo's ideas, Newton came up with his laws of motion. He put his ideas in a book called *The Principia*. He wrote it in Latin and used lots of complicated formulas, because he didn't want "little smatterers" (amateurs in math) to read it. Despite the popular myth, Newton did not get his ideas about gravity from an apple falling on his head.

Weird But True . . .

- To study how vision works, the ever-curious Newton once shoved a large blunt needle under his eyeball.

ALBERT EINSTEIN (1879–1955)

Einstein is as famous for his wild hair as for his radical ideas in physics. In 1905, when he was twenty-six, Einstein published four papers that changed science forever. One of these papers presented his theory of relativity, about the relationship of space and time. It featured his equation $E=MC^2$. In his spare time, Einstein loved to play violin (especially Mozart), sail (though he didn't know how to swim), hike, and tell jokes. When a reporter once asked him a tricky question, he answered, "I am no Einstein!"

Weird But True . . .

- Einstein hated wearing socks, even to fancy dinners. He complained that they easily got holes in them.

GLOSSARY

atoms super tiny building blocks that make up all matter; they are much too small to see.

center of gravity (also called center of mass) the spot where all the weight of an object is centered; the lower an object's center of gravity, the easier it is to balance it.

centripetal force the force that makes an object moving on a curved path keep turning as it goes around. It keeps riders in their seats as they go around a roller coaster loop.

chain reaction what happens when the kinetic energy of an object causes the potential energy of another object to be released. When a row of dominoes topples over one at a time, this is a chain reaction.

conductors materials that let electricity or heat easily pass through them.

electron a negatively charged particle that moves around the outer edges of an atom; when electrons flow from one atom to another, it causes electricity.

first law of motion (also known as **the law of inertia)** Isaac Newton's principle that says that moving objects keep moving, in a straight line at the same speed, unless a force slows them down or speeds them up or makes them change direction. It also says still objects will *not* move unless a force makes them.

friction the force that resists motion when two objects rub together.

gravity an invisible force that pulls all objects in the universe toward one another. The more massive and closer an object is, the more pulling power it has.

implosion when an object collapses in on itself because the pressure pushing in is greater than the pressure pushing out.

inertia Isaac Newton's idea that says that moving objects keep moving, and still objects remain still, unless some force slows or speeds up the object.

insulators materials that help contain heat or electricity.

kinetic energy the type of energy that describes a moving object (the opposite of potential energy).

magnetic field the area around a magnet or magnetized object where the pulling and pushing affect happens.

nucleation the process by which ice crystals form. These crystals form fastest when there's another crystal or impurity to grow on.

nucleus the dense center of an atom that contains protons and neutrons.

pendulum something that swings back and forth from a fixed point—like a playground swing.

permanent magnet a magnet made of a material that is magnetic all the time.

potential energy stored energy that can be released (the opposite of kinetic energy).

prism a multi-surfaced, clear object that can separate white light into all the colors of the rainbow.

refract when light bends due to a change in speed, such as when light traveling in the air bends as it begins to travel through water.

second law of motion Isaac Newton's idea that the speed that a moving object will travel depends on two things: (1) how heavy it is (its mass) and (2) how much force is put on it.

spectrum a band of colors, as seen in a rainbow, that is produced by light being separated according to wavelength.

surface tension a force produced on the surface of a liquid by the molecules that make up that liquid pressing together.

temporary magnet a type of magnet that can be turned "on" or "off" with electricity or by being close to a permanent magnet.

third law of motion Isaac Newton's idea that for every action, there is an equal and opposite reaction. The more force that is used to pull back a flexible object, the greater the amount of force that will be released when the flexible object is let go.

total internal reflection what happens when a beam of light gets trapped in and bounces around in a stream of water or glass tube.

INDEX

"There are only two ways to live your life. One is as though nothing is a miracle. The other is as though everything is a miracle." —Albert Einstein

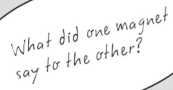

"If I have seen further than others, it is by standing upon the shoulders of giants." —Sir Isaac Newton